DEAREST DAD

A TRIBUTE TO MY DAD

DEBANJAN ROY

Dedicated to the sacred memory of my Baba (Dad) Late Debi Prosad Roy, Maa (Mom) Late Shubhra Roy and my revered Guru, Late Archana Puri Maa of Sree Satyananda Devayatan (Kolkata).

None of them is now on this earth. But I have the strongest faith that they are always with me and guiding me at every moment of my life.

So, it is an honour to humbly submit my offering at their lotus feet and seek their blessings.

My pranam to each one of them!

(Please note: Pranam, a Sanskrit word, stands for 'offering homage'.)

Contents

Prayers vii

A Treasured Memory Of My Family ix

Preface xi

A Candid Confession xiii

Reason Of Penning This Memoir xv

1. A Bit Of Background 1
2. Collage Of Memories 5
3. Glimpse Into A Noble Character 7
4. Some Lovable Quirks 17
5. The Halo Of Golden Virtues 21
6. A Lasting Legacy 25
7. A Concluding Line Of Gratitude 30

An Open Admission Of Divine Help 31

If I Could Just Turn The Clock Back... 33

Prayers

God is Maa, our Divine Mother.

Maa! Pranam at Your lotus feet!

Maa! Please guide us at all times!

Maa! May we ever walk on Your righteous path in life!

Maa! May we always treasure our jewels in life called "Our Parents"!

Pranam to Maa!

A Treasured Memory Of My Family

Seated: Baba(Dad), Maa(Mom) & Standing: Didi(Sister), A Relative and Myself

Location: Garden of Our Home, Delhi (1985)

Preface

Friends, this book is a very personal narrative. It is a reminiscence of my dear Baba (Dad), who passed away on 10th April, 1999 and has now been gone from my life for more than two decades.

Yet, as the days pass by, I find his treasured memories growing stronger and stronger in my mind. It is an intimate feeling, not really amenable to being put down on paper in black and white - it can only be perceived at a very individual level.

To give a brief background, it was during the lockdown period of April- June 2020, that I received divine inspiration from Maa (I call God as Maa, our Divine Mother). An urge grew within to start writing a few lines in the memory of departed Baba. I finally began on 7th June of that year and finished about two weeks later.

Initially, this memoir was an unstructured narrative - it just captured a personal collage of raw emotions, hiding within me for a very long period. Later on, I gave it a shape under the Divine guidance of Maa.

And so far, this narrative has been nestling within the pages of my diary. But now, I have decided to go public with it, despite being aware that some of the contents do not paint me in a good light. The objective is that something here will resonate within your heart, and help you to strengthen your bonds with your own father, something I wish I could have done myself much better in Baba's life-time. Afterall, our father is the rarest of the rare jewel in our lives. The book, you hold in your hand right now, is an outcome of this thought process.

To those of you, who are as unfortunate as I am in losing your father early in life, I offer my sincere condolences and would like to reassure you that your father is always with you, though he may no longer be present in the physical form. Just remember that his blessings will always guide you forward as you chart the course of your own life.

And, to those of you, who are lucky enough to have your father with you right now, it is my earnest request that you cherish the time with him as much as possible. Remember, this treasured period will keep spreading the fragrance of its sweetness and affection in all the days of your life to come.

With Regards,
Debanjan
Dated: 10th April, 2022

A Candid Confession

Among the difficult tasks in the world, penning the memoirs of one's departed parent is possibly the most painful one. While growing-up, our parents are the most reassuring elements in this unpredictable life of ours. That is why, the possibility that one day, they would no longer be around, simply does not enter our reckoning!

And to even contemplate such an eventuality, is something, that is fraught with fear! But alas! Life is never a bed of roses nor will it ever be! Rather, sharp thorns of pain wait at every corner to make us bleed with agony! And the greatest agony in life, unarguably, is the loss of our parents.

I went through this terrible ordeal on the afternoon of 10th April, 1999 when my Baba passed away at around 1:30 PM in the afternoon. It was an evil Saturday that had snatched him away. I remember that date very well, though more than two decades have passed since then.

And before proceeding any further, I must straightaway assert that I have become a staunch believer in Maa, our Divine Mother and always seek Her guidance in all walks of life. So, just as I began writing this memoir, I got a divine flash in my mind. It was Maa sternly cautioning me that I need to be absolutely truthful while penning down this account. And I had to heed Her divine command.

So, obeying that strict warning from Maa, I have to publicly confess with shame that, I was truly not too sorry to have lost Baba on that day in 1999, as it seemed to have come as deliverance from decade-long sufferings!

It needs to be mentioned here that Baba had suffered the scourge of multiple brain strokes way back in 1990 (when I was just 17 years old) and since then, had been rendered just a shell of his former glorious self. His memory was substantially lost, with one side of his body rendered semi-paralysed. For me, as the only son, it used to be heart-rending when he could not even recognize me at times! I would not like to go into any more painful detail. And, this devastating ailment continued for the next ten years continuously!

My mother, another role model in my life, used to care for Baba in the best possible manner and stoically bear all her suffering. The way she nursed him devotedly for ten years at a stretch just brings tears to my eyes...and now, she is gone too!

But what about me??

I have to publicly disclose my shameful attitude then: I used to often think, when others in my age group (17 – 25 years) were all enjoying their lives, how unjust it was that I was saddled with the burden of a permanently sick father forever! Oof! The time has come to openly acknowledge this despicably self-centred attitude of mine! ...And the time has come for me to publicly admit that there were actual moments when I had longed for release from such a burden!

Let all readers take a lesson from me and learn to mend their thoughts about their parents well in time...else, the pangs of the inevitable self-remorse that sets in during the middle-age are just indescribable, as I am finding now!

Oh, Maa!

Do forgive me!

Have mercy on me!

Have pity on this sinner!

Reason Of Penning This Memoir

In the section on "Confessions", I have openly given vent to the dark emotional state of mine during Baba's decade-long illness that had robbed him of his former golden persona.

Yes! Baba had an absolutely beautiful self which I was privileged to witness and be a part of! Anyone, who had ever come into contact with him, will attest to this. So, the most important reason for penning this memoir is pretty personal. And it is simply this: I want to just relive those gloriously joyful times I had spent under the loving care of an affectionate Baba.

Indeed, in hindsight, my growing-up period from 1976 to 1988 seems to be idyllic in character vis-à-vis my adult life now and by penning the pages to follow, I wish to revive the beautiful memories of those delightful days once more!

So, here we start on this nostalgic journey of evergreen memories...

CHAPTER I

A Bit of Background

For the benefit of readers, I am sharing a short life sketch of my dear Baba here:

Birth

My Baba, Sri Debi Prasad Roy was born on the 5th of June, 1935 at a village in the district of Medinipur in undivided Bengal. This place, located near the town of Jhargram, is filled with great natural beauty even now. Green meadows, rolling forest, sparkling streams, expansive blue sky - all these elements come together to lend unparalleled scenic beauty! And I believe, when Baba was born, these forests were much more sense and served as home for the great cats such as tigers as well! And, herds of wild elephants are found here even now.

Childhood Hardships

Baba was born to Sri Kalyan Prasad Roy and Srimati Ashalata Roy in a family of six other siblings. I have heard from 'Pisi' (my paternal aunt) that the eldest child, a son had passed away in infancy itself. Then came Kumari Bela Roy(late), followed by Kumari Ila Roy(late) with Baba coming as a third child. Next, three sons were born – Sri Jayanta Prasad Roy(late), Sri Soumen Chandra Roy and Sri Samir Chandra Roy in that order.

So, the family headed by Sri Kalyan Prasad Roy, as head of the family, comprised of two daughters and four sons.

Here my lasting regret is that I did not have the good fortune of seeing my Grandpa alive: he had already passed away before I was born. So, I have to satisfy myself only with his photographs.

However, I count my blessings as I could see my grandma alive - she was a sweet lady with a tender nature. We used to call her as 'Amma' – I clearly recollect that she was very pious, spending a large proportion of her time in worship and prayers. Probably, I have imbibed that quality now.

When Baba was born, India was still a British colony: in those times only a narrow section of the society was well-off and the rest of the society was mired in economic hardships. My grandpa's family belonged to the second strata and hence, my Baba's childhood was spent amidst great financial difficulties. Earning a respectable livelihood was a quite tough proposition in a backward village in those colonial times of the 1930s and 1940s. (For this reason, I feel so grateful to Baba now: he had to struggle so much in childhood yet always fought hard to keep his own family in comfort later on!)

Thus, unrelenting monetary hardships made my Grandpa migrate, along with his entire family, from Jhargram to Kolkata in the 1950's. In this City, the family had first sought refuge in Roop Chand Mukherjee lane in the Bhawanipur locality and then, in Jadavpur in the southern part.

It was a time of great struggle for the family to make ends meet and at the same time, ensure a decent education for all the six children. As the eldest son, Baba had to shoulder a large part of those deprivations: he had to do lots of tuition and other odd jobs, thereby sacrificing his own education and career for the sake of his family.

Such relentless battle from a young age made my father a self-sufficient man in adulthood. Therefore, I have now come to develop tremendous admiration for Baba: he was the very definition of a self-made man from the word go!

Education

My Baba had completed his schooling from Jhargram itself. However, the place did not have much scope for good education. Indeed, this was true for most of rural Bengal! And so, a search for better educational infrastructure was one of the additional reasons, that had made my Grandpa migrate with his family to Kolkata.

Thereafter, my Baba completed his graduation from the reputed institution of Ashutosh College in Kolkata. To his great credit, Baba later on completed the ICWA (Institute of Cost and Works Accountants of India) membership, when he was already into his middle ages, bearing the heavy burden of a full family. And, before illness intervened, he even wanted to pursue the tough course of ICSI (Institute of Company Secretary of India) membership as well!

Thus, he had a great life-long hunger for education: this was one of his many sterling qualities! In the hindsight, I'm just fascinated by the constant learning zeal of Baba all through his life! Baba, I'm so proud of you!

Immediate Family and Service Life

Baba and Maa were blessed by a daughter in 1966 and then, a son in 1973. He had begun his career in Kolkata in 1960's. And afterwards, he had shifted to New Delhi in 1976, when he joined a Central Government Undertaking there in their Accounts Department.

The gloriously happy days of my boyhood period were spent in the lovely family accommodation allotted to Baba in the nice Staff Colony of this last Organization. He remained in service here till 1990, when cerebral stroke overtook him and forced him into voluntary retirement and hence, return to Kolkata.

The Mortal End

Baba passed away on Saturday, the 10th April, 1999 in Kolkata. Thus, curtains came down on the pole star of my life at the relatively early age of 63 years.

He may have thus left more than two decades ago but his memory is ever-present in my heart!

Oh, Baba! How much I miss you now!

"No matter how tall a son grows, he will always look up to his dad." – Anonymous

CHAPTER II

Collage of Memories

We have seen in the preceding paragraphs how the fire of hardships forged my Baba into a 'Man of Steel': that was his inner core. And now, I invite the readers on a nostalgic journey, as I touch upon some of my fond memories of Baba as a person.

His Physical Appearance

My earliest memory of Baba goes back to around 1977 when I was around 3.5 years old. From that age onward, my memory is quite distinct. And what I clearly remember is that Baba looked quite tall and imposing to a small child of that age! He was tall indeed at 5 feet 11 inches in height! And to boot, he looked well-built too.

I recollect his going to the badminton courts with racquets: he had the matching physique of a player. Indeed, in his prime, he was a handsome man with a face topped by a thick mop of black hair stylishly back-brushed, and a slim body: this is borne out by his photographs taken on stage while acting in amateur theatre! He was a man of many parts indeed!

I also recall he had a dusky complexion that used to stand in sharp contrast to the pristine white shirts he used to wear to his office every day. And blessed with a pair of twinkling eyes and a lovely smile, that frequently used to brighten his expressive face, I just used to love him madly!

His Personality

Stated in the simplest words, my Baba had an engaging personality. As a small child, the very first thing I recall was his affectionate nature: he used to just shower his love on his children in boundless measure.

Now, how much do I love to recollect his tender voice calling out to me by my pet-name, 'Babu'! And in my glowing memory, I simply prize those occasions, when in response to my addressing him as 'Baba', he would affectionately call me back as 'Baba' too!! It is a beauty of culture in our Bengal that parents affectionately address their small sons and daughters as 'Baba' and 'Maa' respectively.

His Favourite Saying

He loved to tell us quite often, "Why should I fear work? It is the work that has to fear me!"

In other words, he was a person who never flinched from any duty that came his way: he was simply a role-model in more ways than one!

"The greatest gift I ever had, came from God; I call him Father." – Anonymous

CHAPTER III

Glimpse into a Noble Character

Writing this memoir has made me introspect quite often. And more and more, I've come to realize some of the wonderful qualities that had graced Baba's personality. So, let us now have a peek into them and uplift ourselves:

Organising Excellence

Baba had an unmatched ability to organize! He had superb planning skills, with a matching aptitude for implementation!

In the planning arena, Baba had an excellent knack for visualising the events likely to take place in future and then planning well ahead in time. Here, he had been blessed with the ability to see the larger picture as well as the smaller details, at the same time.

And in execution ability, Baba just came into his own colours! He had an exceptional ability to get things done on the ground level. He was marvellously adept at multitasking and coordinating with others as well.

Example:

Now, let me share an instance of the organising excellence of Baba, as seen from the eyes of his small son. When I was a child in the 5-9 years age bracket, I used to get just fascinated seeing how smoothly Baba would organise our annual railway trips!

Every year, Shyama Prasad Vidyalaya (the wonderful school where my sister and myself were studying together in Delhi) would close for summer vacation during May-

June and accordingly, Baba would take us by Deluxe Express to Kolkata in early-May. And after happily spending our vacations there and at Dhanbad(my maternal home), we would return to Delhi in end-June, in time for the new session of our school. Baba would return earlier.

Now, there used to be a huge rush in trains on Delhi-Howrah route in the summer season and so, Baba would plan our trip several months ahead of the actual date of journey and book the tickets accordingly.

And then, the extent of organising excellence of Baba used to come into the full display! I used to raptly witness how methodically Baba used to go about packing our voluminous luggage down to the last detail! And then I'll be captivated once more, when he would so deftly move our family with its heavy luggage, from our Delhi home by taxi to New Delhi Railway Station and then onto the designated platform, a full hour before the scheduled departure of Howrah-bound Deluxe Express!

Thanks to Baba's single-handed organizing ability, such overnight train journeys used to be such a pleasurable experience! He used to be so meticulous in taking care of each and every aspect: loading our luggage into the train at New Delhi Railway Station, serving our meals, supervising our sleeping arrangements, making us comfortable, unloading the luggage at Howrah Railway Station, and then finally, transporting everyone with everything by taxi to grandmother's place in Kolkata!

To someone else, all these may sound quite commonplace but to a small child, my Baba used to look like no less than a magician, who could so wonderfully ensure that each and everything was at the right place at the right time!

Aw Baba! I truly miss your magic touch!

Gardening Talent

Baba's excellent gardening talent was just beyond compare! So, allow me to gleefully plunge into this blissful memory.

In the introduction, I have stated that Baba was brought up in a village in the very lap of Mother Nature. Thus, he grew up with a love for greenery in his very blood and this love came into full bloom when he was allotted family accommodation in the form of a nice bungalow in the Staff Colony of his employing Organization in Delhi.

Now, this bungalow was blessed with ample space for gardening on all three sides: the front, the right side and the back. So, utilizing his great organizing ability, Baba systematically planned the layout of the garden of our house.

First, the front space was selected to house a flower garden and a grass lawn - that would really enhance the beauty of our house later on. Then, Baba arranged to utilise the large space to the right by laying out a model vegetable garden. Finally, he decided to have a fruit orchard in the space at the back.

This vegetable garden truly showed that Baba had the proverbial green thumb! Utilising his phenomenal planning expertise, he initially chose which vegetables he would grow in which season.

Here it is worth briefly touching upon the climate in Delhi in 1980's: this Capital city would have a long Summer season from April to July, when the rains would start. The temperature would start falling in September to begin the onset of Autumn lasting till October. Afterwards, the famous Winter season of Delhi would start, which would be there till February. And the month of March would be blessed with the lovely Spring.

For growing vegetables, the best season was the winter. So, Baba would utilize this season to full by planting seeds and saplings of a wide range of vegetables such as cauliflower, cabbage, mustard greens, carrot, radish, turnip etc. And if I recall correctly, we would have ladies-finger in the Summer and tomatoes in the Spring. I also distinctly remember that Baba used to grow root vegetables such as potatoes and onions too.

Our vegetable garden was comprised of a series of neatly laid-out rectangular plots. And Baba (in consultation with a gardener who used to come to our house occasionally) would decide which vegetables would grow in which plot. In some of the plots, he would get seeds of the selected vegetables planted. Elsewhere, he used to get small saplings of vegetables directly sown. These saplings and seeds used to be sourced from a nearby nursery in the Hazrat Nizamuddin area.

In due course, the seeds would sprout and Baba would begin lovingly looking after the growing plants with daily watering, regular weeding, adding fertilizers and spraying of pesticides, as needed. And the plants would repay their gratitude for such loving care through a bountiful harvest of vegetables!

The beautiful flower garden in the front of our bungalow would be graced by blooms of Spider Lily, Zinnia and Sunflower in Summer while the colourful blossoms of Marigold, Calendula, Chrysanthemum, etc. would grow in profusion during winter. I recollect that the flowering plants of 'Nayantara' would gift us its lovely violet blossoms many times a year. And to add the final touch, the beautiful Indian red rose would bloom in regal splendour during Autumn as well as Spring...what a delightful fragrance it had! This lawn and the flower garden would be guarded by wire mesh with a green hedge, on which tiny flowers would grow.

And at the back, Baba had planted a fruit orchard, where banana, grapes, and guava trees would bear luscious fruits. There was a pre-existing pomegranate tree as well. The guava tree was my favourite as it bore fruits that were sweet and within my reach as well!

Truly, our beautiful garden was the most poetic expression of Baba's love for Mother Nature! It's photographs kindle so many joyful memories now!

A Man of Many Parts

Baba, to his great credit, had a multi-faceted personality that encompassed active interests in sports, music, theatre, photography etc. The very fact that Baba could devote time and energy to pursue these hobbies, despite the harsh struggle for existence undergone by him ever since his birth, speaks volumes for his innate refined taste!

In sports, I had personally witnessed Baba going to take part in outdoor games such as badminton: he used to be quite regular in practice matches. I have also witnessed him engrossed in indoor games like chess. And how avidly he used to watch the Cricket Matches (both Test-series and One-day) and the Tennis Matches (such as Wimbledon) on TV! And I believe, during his youth in Kolkata, he used to personally attend Football Matches between Clubs there. Aha! What a sports lover he was!

In music, Baba had very good tastes: he used to love 'Hindustani Classical Music'. And I remember that Sagar Sen, with his melodious voice and crystal-clear diction, was one of his favourite singers in 'Rabindra Sangeet', whose audio-cassettes would be played by Baba often at home. He would love listening to 'Ghazal' by Jagjit Singh too.

I also have heard that, during his stay in Jadavpur in Kolkata, Baba used to regularly take part in amateur theatre, organized during the annual Durga Puja celebrations in the locality. He was blessed with a good voice, and a fine physique and was quite expressive as well: all these qualities had combined to make Baba into a fine amateur actor! Alas! All these had happened before my birth and so, I had to always remain content, by just watching black and white photographs of Baba, acting on stage.

And last but not the least, he was good in photography as well: in this art, he was self-taught, just like everywhere else. So many albums at home still bear silent testimony to his talent.

So, taking all things into account, I'm simply honoured to declare: Baba was indeed a man of many parts!!

Culinary Talent

One quality, that I always used to deeply admire in Baba, was his childlike curiosity about new things: he was always eager to try out something new every time.

This extended to the arena of his eating habits as well: he was a connoisseur of good food and this used to prompt him to experiment with cooking new dishes from time to time.

As a child, how deeply I used to cherish those special treats of Baba! I still lovingly reminisce about Baba getting a Chinese cookbook, which I used to love reading like a novel! And what a great enthusiasm he used to display in the kitchen, while organizing all the ingredients such as Soy sauce, Ajinomoto etc. for a sumptuous Chinese feast!

Baba also used to regularly try his hand at preparing new Bengali delicacies and snacks. I believe he had also prepared the Mughlai dish of Biryani several times. Just how yummy those dishes used to be...!

Delhi summers are notorious for their extremes: I am grateful to Baba and Maa for helping us to beat the heat through their homemade ice creams, milk shakes and mango shakes - all so lip-smacking to taste!

And I'm proud to say that the flavours of all such home-made delicacies linger in the memory even after the passage of so many decades...after all, the main ingredient in each dish was love!!

A Comic event related to Baba's cooking:

I recall a comic incident that took place in connection with the cooking of new dishes by Baba. One particular year, our generous vegetable garden produced a bountiful harvest of tomatoes. At that point in time, our lovable granny (called Amma by all her grandchildren) was the treasured guest at home.

Now Amma used to be a very good cook: she immediately went about cooking a special style of curry from those raw tomatoes almost every day. But sadly, the huge number of tomatoes being plucked from the garden soon outgrew even Amma's phenomenal capacity to manage!

It was at that point of time Baba stepped in. With a dramatic flourish, he declared that he would prepare homemade tomato "ketchup" from the excess tomatoes! Filled with great zeal, he displaced both Amma and Maa from the kitchen...and after checking on the recipe of how to prepare tomato ketchup, he picked up a huge cooking pan, placed it on the gas stove burner, added all the necessary ingredients and then earnestly commenced on "mission tomato ketchup", as rest of the family waited with great anticipation!

Alas! Due to the excess of one ingredient, most probably vinegar, the taste of the end-product was quite interesting, to put it mildly! And to put it bluntly, it was extremely sour! I still remember, with loving fondness, Baba's sheepish admission, "Well, this homemade tomato "ketchup" seems to have a different taste!"

In the end, all that home-made "ketchup" had to be used up by Maa in her regular cooking over the next few months...and she was not happy about it at all! The net result was that Baba was banished by Maa from the kitchen for quite some time!

Poor Baba! I must confess that my sister and myself thoroughly enjoyed the whole episode from the safety of side-lines! Haha!

And, even after the passage of so many decades, the sweet memory of this event lingers...Oh! Baba, miss you so much!

An Icon of Joy

One of the prime elements in Baba's character, that made him so popular with everybody, was his abundant sense of humour.

The best display of that element was his ever-smiling nature. Now and then, he flashed a very sweet smile: I treasure that smile of his till this date! At other times, he used to break out in a burst of deep belly laughter on encountering anything hilarious. And this laughter used to make others to laugh with him too!

Baba used to have a keen sense of observation and I believe his talent as an amateur actor had enabled him to observe the habits of the persons he met and then draw-up humorous caricatures.

Thus, in marriage gatherings, one would find Baba in a centre of a large group of relatives, who would go on helplessly giggling, while he would do one caricature after another! But all these caricatures used to be done by him in the good sense: he took care to never ever hurt anyone on this account.

Baba could also relate jokes with telling effect with appropriate emotions and effective pauses. All of us used to laugh so much hearing his jokes.

I believe an inner current of joy used to always flow inside Baba and animate his whole being: those jolly vibes used to give happiness to others as well!

In a nutshell, Baba was a true icon of joy!

Neatness of Habit

I distinctly remember that Baba used to be immaculate as well as methodical in his approach to daily life - I guess this was his inherent nature.

This used to become very clear from the way he used to neatly arrange his office files and stationery on the table, keep the clothes neatly arranged in the almirah, fold clothes while packing suitcases for train journey, ensure placement of the garden implements at the right place, take care of his scooter, observe punctuality in his life and ... the list virtually goes on...! And what stylish handwriting he had, including the neat way in which he used to sign his name in full!

Truly, this neatness of daily habits is one of my sweetest memories of Baba!

"Life doesn't come with an instruction book—that's why we have fathers." – H Jackson Browne

CHAPTER IV

Some Lovable Quirks

So far, I have touched upon the qualities of Baba. Now, every human being has got some typical quirks in his personality and Baba was no exception to this rule. With a great deal of affection, I am placing a few of them here.

A Fondness for Food

Stated in simple terms, Baba was a food lover. This enabled him to relish with delight the nutritious meals, my mother served us at home, every day. And, on the other hand, he could also enjoy with gusto, all the delicacies served in dinners of traditional Bengali wedding receptions. I have heard Baba competed with another relative regarding who could eat more of the famous Bengali sweet delicacy, rosogolla in one such dinner! (it was during late 1970's and I am not too sure of the details as I was very small then.)

In addition, I also recall with a smile on my lips how Baba would periodically bring meals from Chinese take-aways: both me and my sister would eagerly look forward to such delicious treats! And, at other times, he would bring home dishes of Mughlai cuisine such as 'rumali roti', 'naan', 'paneer' etc.

Sometimes, Baba would take his whole family to a Chinese restaurant or a Punjabi restaurant for dinner, particularly when all of us used to go to the Central Market in Lajpat Nagar in South Delhi. Here it is worth mentioning that, normally at our home, mother would always eat last – she would take her meal only after ensuring that Baba, myself and sister had been fed. So, these restaurant dinners used to be those rare occasions in Delhi when all four of us: Baba, Maa, sister and myself would eat together. Now, that I have lost both Baba and Maa, such memories are just priceless to me!

And I have already described his culinary talents earlier. All in all, this was a very lovable characteristic of Baba.

Aversion to Cold

In an earlier section, I have referred to the extremes of weather in Delhi. This Capital city, situated bang in the middle of the northern plains (and hence, far away from the moderating influence of the sea), experiences extreme climates throughout the year. For example, this city is boilingly hot in the summer, and in sharp contrast, bitterly cold in the winter.

And when I was a child in Delhi, the winter season used to typically start during the end-October and peak in mid-December, with the maximum temperature during the day registering 17 degrees Celsius (compared to the summer maximum of 45 degrees Celsius) and the minimum temperature at night falling to as low as 4 degrees celsius! And this chill would continue till mid-January! Such weather used to be aggravated by the bitterly cold northern winds, with the sun being hidden under clouds for days together!

Now, our family had migrated to Delhi in 1976 when I was just 3 years old. So I had quickly got acclimatised to the cold of Delhi's winters as children have a very good ability to adapt. And since my mother was born and brought up in Dhanbad and then educated in the towns of Ranchi and Patna, all in the state of Bihar, she too was accustomed to the bitter cold of winter in Bihar!

Alas! It was a completely different case for Baba! He had been born and brought up in Bengal, which has much more moderate weather, thanks to its proximity to the sea. So, for Baba, Delhi's climate proved to be a shocker: especially its winter was just too much for him!

Thus, the peak of Delhi's winter would see Baba fully wrapped in layers and layers of wooden clothes from head to toe! And his face would be protectively hidden under a muffler, his upper body would be ensconced under a couple of sweaters, his feet would be protected under socks, and sometimes for additional protection, there would be an artistic Kashmiri overcoat on top of everything!

At times, especially during end-December and early-January, even all such protections would not suffice! Then he would come home straight from the office, don all his protective gear, and establish himself securely before a blazing room heater inside a room with all windows closed! Sometimes, just to make sure that no heat should leak from his room, he would close the internal communication door too!

Such extreme cold-aversion used to be a sight to behold and a source of amusement to me! And as if to prove this point, he used to normally refrain from venturing outside the home in the evenings in the peak of winter, unless called out by duty. He would usually return straight from the office and then stay home, come what may!

Alas! Now that he is no more, all such scenes flash before my eyes! Those days would never return! And now it really pains me to imagine his difficulties in the harsh winter of Delhi. As a child, I was immature but as an adult now, I have grown full empathy for his difficulties.

In the end, one more important point remains to be stated, and this point speaks volumes about the golden character of Baba. And this point is that Baba was a man whose hallmark was simplicity. Thus, he always had just a few clothes to wear and this was true for his woollens also. So, despite the intensity of Delhi's cold and his own susceptibility to that, he would remain content with just a few pieces of warm clothing!

All such memories just bring tears in my eyes now! Oh Baba! I just miss your simplicity! This golden quality of yours is so scarce in these artificial times of today!

Belief in Astrology

One such quirk Baba had, was a belief in the stars - he used to consult astrologers on different occasions. I can now distinctly recall that he used to wear gemstones prescribed by astrologers in his finger rings. And as a child, I was particularly fascinated by the red gemstone on his ring!

Much later, after he had passed away, I happened to discover a few horoscopes one day. On study, I found that Baba had got them made for himself and his two children: me and my sister. I also discovered notes in his handwriting in those papers: the sight of his neat handwriting, made decades ago in the 1980s, immediately drove me to tears!

Oh! how much I miss Baba now!

"For thousands of years, father and son have stretched wistful hands across the canyon of time." - Alan Valentine

CHAPTER V

The Halo of Golden Virtues

More than two decades have passed since the day Baba left us forever. Now, as I spend more and more time reflecting, his character started glittering before me in its true light. So, let me offer homage by a study of his magnificent virtues and in the process, elevate myself as well.

Active Nature

Baba could most appropriately be described by the adjective "active" from the word go. He was an energetic person - never sitting idle - always taking initiative - always on the move. At any place and hour, he would be found engaged in some form of productive work.

In fact, he used to thoroughly dislike passivity in any form. For example, if he ever found me in bed lying idly, he used to ask me at once, "Babu, are you not feeling well?" Being an active person, lying in bed unnecessarily, would be tantamount to being unwell for him!

Now-a-days, most of us grumble when we have to carry out various boring yet necessary chores of daily life. But Baba was never a man to shy away from any such mundane task nor display any negative attitude about it. He used to just wholeheartedly plunge into the task!

A simple example would suffice: in the Jangpura locality of Delhi (where we used to stay), the market was located quite a distance away from our residential complex. But any typical day would find Baba rushing to the market on his scooter at least once. And at the time of visits of our relatives, such marketing forays would occur multiple times a day. Yet, each time he returned home, Baba would actively look out for the next opportunity of giving service!

Another place that bore the unmistakable mark of his active nature was our spacious garden. He used to regularly put-up loving toil there, especially in our kitchen garden. This included his frequent journeys to the nursery to get seeds, saplings, fertilizer etc. And then the harvests of vegetables would bear bountiful testimony to his hard work!

Then, as already mentioned, at railway platforms, despite his age, he never shied away from lifting and carrying heavy pieces of luggage without waiting for any assistance. At marriage celebrations and other family gatherings, he would always be found lending a helping hand. At Office, he used to work hard. And he used to play hard on badminton courts as well!

In a nutshell, wherever he was, he was up doing something useful always. All in all, Baba was the very personification of the wonderful trait called 'industriousness'!

A People's Person

Baba was an ideal epitome of a people's person. From my earliest childhood, I witnessed that he used to love mingling with people. He was a gregarious man given to jolly laughter and making others laugh along with him as well.

I recall that he had innate consideration for others and was blessed with a very good listening ability. For example, I could blindly trust that he would lend a patient ear to me, whenever I used to rush to him with any issue at any hour.

Such consideration for others made him truly a gem of a person! How rare these qualities have become now!

And one more aspect comes to my mind in the above context: in any large gathering of people like marriage celebrations, Baba would invariably become the centre of attention: people would love to gather around him and hear his jokes and anecdotes raptly! And shortly, everyone would be rolling in laughter and merriment. What a joyous personality he had!

One more feather used to grace the crown of his generosity: his wonderful hospitality! He used to love hosting our out-station relatives when they used to visit us and stay with us for some time. They included both my maternal as well as paternal relatives. And from the time Baba used to receive them at Delhi Railway Station to the time he would bid them farewell, he would be the ever-gracious host, who looked after the needs of his guests with utmost attentiveness.

It needs to be mentioned that this would also include bringing delicacies from different food takeaways...Aha! How delicious those dishes were! So, as a child, I used to relish these visits by our relatives to our home, thanks to the wonderful display of hospitality by Baba!

Contentment

Contentment was one of the brightest hallmarks of Baba's sterling character. I can recognise this fact only now as I introspect on the days gone by. He used to spend so little on himself: most of his earnings used to be earmarked for his family!

Thus, he owned just a few clothes: a few good shirts and trousers to wear to the office, a few vests and 'lungi' (a traditional lower garment worn by males in India) to don inside the home and only a few sweaters to wear in the winter! He used to smilingly pass his days like this!

Baba used to teach this value to others too. In fact, he used to regularly counsel me: “Babu, you must learn to eat whatever is served to you”. He used to convey this message if I threw any tantrum over food at home.

Baba used to be content with the simple pleasures afforded by family life. I distinctly remember him returning from his office in the evening and then patiently playing ‘Ludo’ with his small children with a great deal of happiness. He liked to spend time at home in the simple pleasures of chess and gardening and did not care for outings to movies etc.

For his commuting, Baba was content with just a simple two-wheeler: initially, a ‘Luna’ moped and then, a ‘Bajaj Chetak; scooter. And as far as holidays were concerned, he was content to travel to Kolkata and spend time with Amma there. Thus, Baba was just ‘contentment’ personified.

The Message of His Life:

So, it speaks volumes for his character that, despite being dealt with so many blows by life, Baba always preserved his basic magnanimous nature and kept on helping people - wherever he could - whenever he could - in whatever way he could! I feel just so honoured to pen his memoir!

"A son’s first hero is his Father." – Anonymous

CHAPTER VI

A Lasting Legacy

Since the time I decided to offer homage to Baba in writing, I have grown to be more and more contemplative. This inner process has led to my serendipitous realization about his wonderful legacy for us – something that is infinitely richer than any earthly asset - and that is an extraordinarily meaningful set of Values.

As I write this account on 20th June 2020, I'm wonder-struck by the fact that Baba has been gone for more than two decades; yet this priceless heirloom he left for us has stood the test of time and lives on. Hence, a respectful study of such Values is sure to elevate each one of us:

A Strong Positive Attitude Towards Life

Baba had to overcome tremendous odds in life, and yet he came out as a winner in the end. Though born very poor, he was the very definition of self-made man in his adulthood. In other words, he received very little help from life but achieved a lot, in my eyes.

And how did he manage to achieve this feat? Well, as I see it, he accomplished this by:

- Calmly accepting his lot,
- Then, stoically accepting all the duties, big or small, that fell upon his strong shoulders at various stages of life,
- Silently discharging all such responsibilities to the best of his ability without ever uttering a single word of complaint against his fate.

- And last but not the least, learning continuously and striving to add to his educational qualifications all through his life, so that he could provide for his family better.

What a role model he was! What a fighting spirit he had! And what perseverance he had to keep up his learning zeal till the very end!

Baba, I'm just so proud of you!

A Spirit of Selflessness

For Baba, the welfare of others always came before his own. He constantly lived this value in his life and became an excellent example to follow regarding how to treat his family, relatives, friends, colleagues, neighbours and society in general, with basic human decency, at all times. Helping others came naturally to him.

Simplicity

If someone had the good fortune to meet Baba even once, he would have surely been struck with a simplicity that shone through him; he would have assuredly seen a simple, ever-smiling man, content with little but always ready to help others.

Hard work

Through his own life, Baba taught us that life is not a bed of roses and that, you have to meet its challenges head-on. He constantly upheld the value of toil in life and by his own conduct, demonstrated how not to fall prey to the twin set of very common human failings: laziness and procrastination.

I am of the firm opinion that, if anyone imbibes this one single value, his life is bound to get transformed. Because then, he would learn to take initiative in life and thus, become proactive. And being proactive is one of the highest virtue a man can aspire to.

The Attitude of 'Shraddha' (Respect and Gratitude)

Baba was a person, who was always deeply reverential towards Mother Nature and all the resources She granted us. While, sadly, the majority of us remain uncaring and ungrateful, Baba was a golden exception: he deeply cared for everything that came his way.

Born amidst great economic hardships in a backward village in a remote area, Baba came to deeply respect Mother Nature while growing up. In fact, something much greater underlay this: it was his attitude of gratitude! He was deeply grateful for anything given to him or made by him or purchased by him.

Hence, he automatically took great care to use such things in the most optimal manner possible. This was his own way of showing reverence to Mother Nature and all the facilities She grants her children. In a nutshell, Baba was filled with the divine virtue of "Shraddha".

That is why, he laid so much stress upon daily conservation of water, doing gardening to grow our own vegetables, conservation of electricity through optimum use of domestic appliances, judicious use of articles of daily use so that everything can last long, showing respect to time through punctual habits, giving due reverence to

Goddess of Wealth through the habit of compulsory savings, cultivating manners and etiquettes in daily conduct ... the list just goes on!

For the rest of us, who are born amidst plenty, and who often take many things for granted, this is an extremely important value to imbibe and then, constantly practice in our own lives.

Magnanimity

Baba had a wonderfully generous and forgiving nature. He never kept any grudge festering in his heart and was readily forgiving of all the mistakes and follies of others. This was because he was deeply conscious of the frailties of human character. And therefore, he was able to keep himself mostly free from the completely unnecessary burden of hatred and revenge-mongering, that stains so many human hearts.

Summary of Baba's Legacy

The aforementioned account, though hardly able to do justice to the task of adequately describing the Value-System of Baba, gives at least an inkling of the kind of man he was. These Values are eternal and served as a bedrock for the noble character he had.

And therein lies his legacy: he silently taught us how to lead a life of honour as a self-made person. He taught us how to be content with so little, yet give so much, by radiating positivity all around him.

In a nutshell, the lasting achievement of Baba's life is that he taught us how to live our own lives in a humane manner. And through the everlasting Values of his character, his teaching continues to cast its beneficial influence over me till this day and will continue ever after!

"Daddies don't just love their children every now and then, it's a love without end." – George Strait

CHAPTER VII

A Concluding Line of Gratitude

As I come to the end of this memoir of Baba, I feel that I have just elevated myself by penning all the preceding pages. As a result, writing this account has been nothing short of an extra-ordinarily meaningful journey of self-introspection for me.

And by delving deeper and deeper into the great personality of Baba, I have just now begun to understand and then, appreciate the wonderful framework of Values that lay beneath his smiling yet steely character. And in the process, his golden standards have shown me the right path to take in my own life.

To sum up, he is the best role-model in the world for me. Baba, I just love you! With these words, I offer my homage to the lotus feet of Baba and humbly offer this account as a tribute to his evergreen memories. For me, he shall dwell alive in my heart forever!

My Pranam to Baba!

An Open Admission Of Divine Help

Maa, our Divine Mother always answers prayers. And it is due to Her blessings that I could hop onto a 'time machine' and go back by decades to those wonderful times of the 1970s and 1980s! Those were my happiest days when I was spending blissful years under the loving wings of my parents!

I am so grateful to Maa because Her Divine blessing of 'time machine' enabled me to thankfully recall all the memories of Baba, as I used to see him as a child all those years ago. And with Her grace, it was the dual process of this constant flashback to my childhood and simultaneous self-reflection as an adult, that silently started revealing the golden character of my Baba. Only due to Her benediction, the hitherto undiscovered deep-seated Values and the Virtues of Baba took shape through my pen, before my own astonished eyes!

And by the time I finished writing his memoir, I found myself submerged under an all-engulfing wave of respect, love and gratitude towards Baba as his unexplored character begin to shine before me in its true light! Thus, I just feel so glad to repeatedly affirm now, "Baba, I love you."

This uplifting wave is a direct blessing of Maa! So, I openly acknowledge that I could write this memoir only because Maa listened to my constant prayers and guided me along the right path.

Maa, Pranam at Your Lotus Feet!

If I Could Just Turn The Clock Back...

An Earnest Wish

If I could turn the clock back, then I would like to tell Baba everyday:

Baba, I love you!

Baba, I'm so proud of you!

Baba, I'm so grateful to you!

Baba, you are the most loving person here on this earth!

Baba, I just want to spend more time with you!

Baba, I want to have your learning spirit!

Baba, I want to be a self-made man like you!

Baba, I want you to teach me how to live like you!

Baba...

And the list simply goes on!

Oh, Maa!

If I could only turn the clock back!

9 798886 679625

Printed by Libri Plureos GmbH in Hamburg, Germany